Fondearest Ly
a happy Easter '93

A
WILD FLOWER
ALPHABET

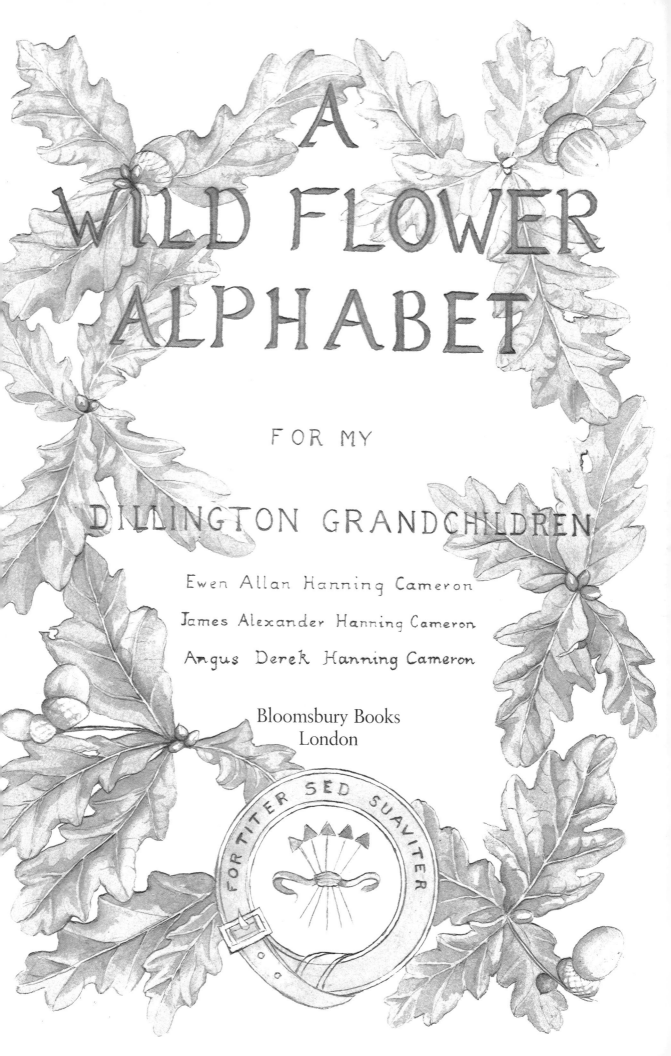

A WILD FLOWER ALPHABET

FOR MY

DILLINGTON GRANDCHILDREN

Ewen Allan Hanning Cameron

James Alexander Hanning Cameron

Angus Derek Hanning Cameron

Bloomsbury Books
London

FORTITER SED SUAVITER

First published in Great Britain 1983 by
Webb & Bower (Publishers) Limited
9 Colleton Crescent, Exeter, Devon EX2 4BY

Copyright © Webb & Bower (Publishers) Limited

This edition published by Bloomsbury Books, an imprint of
Godfrey Cave Associates, 42 Bloomsbury Street, London, WC1B 3QJ,
under licence from Webb & Bower Ltd 1992

Jacket design by Peter Wrigley

British Library Cataloguing in Publication Data
Cameron, Elizabeth, 1915–
  A wild flower alphabet.
  1. Wild flowers—Great Britain
  I. Title
  582.13′0941   QK306

ISBN 1-85471-0-745

Printed and bound in Great Britain by
BPCC Hazells Ltd
Member of BPCC Ltd

Allangrange,

Munlochy

Ross-shire

My Dear Grandchildren,

I first got the idea of making a little ABC picture book of Wild Flowers for you, when your Father said quite rightly that we had rather failed as parents in not teaching them about the nature all around us, such as wild flowers, birds, insects and trees. I then realized how little I knew myself, or had been taught. I knew just a very little about birds, because my Mother pointed out to me, those she knew and I was encouraged to go birdsnesting. Even so her birds did go rather under three headings, Game Birds Water Birds and Dickie Birds; but she did teach me to watch notice and enquire. However wild flowers insects or trees never came much my way, except when my sister and myself were encouraged to collect and press wild flowers by a governess we had for a year or two, and in that time I did learn quite a bit.

Incidently it was this same Governess, Miss Edith Archer, who gave me my first drawing lessons and taught me how to handle water colour lessons I have never forgotten.

Though I only knew very little about wild flowers, I have learnt far more while painting and writing the two books for you and your cousins, than I have learnt ever before. So even if you do not learn overmuch from this book, Grandpa and I certainly have!

You will learn later on at school, if you study Botany, that flowers are divided into families, and within these families there are lots of different flowers – all different, but with family ties, just like your cousins Marion and Rachel have with you.

Perhaps you will be able to start collecting wild flowers when you go for walks and then press them between paper under a heavy weight, or in a flower press if you have one.   If you do not have one suggest some one gives you one for your birthday.   Then stick the pressed flower in a book, and always write underneath the flower, its correct name (once you have discovered what it is) and the date you found it and where you found it.

       We always hear of keen and perhaps rather eccentric gardeners who talk to their flowers, well I hope in this book that the flowers will talk to you, I have tried to make them.

       So here they are. I have finished painting all the pictures now, and have looked them all up, and written a little bit about each one, and Grandpa has transalated my writing into English and adjusted my appalling spelling.   When your mother suggested I should find a little poem for each flower, I thought this was a good idea, but there are lots of poems by lots of real poets (not like me) who write about the popular flowers such as roses, cowslips, pansies, and daisies etc. but no one seems inspired to compose poems about such flowers as Yarrow, Willow herb, or Gorse or King Cups.   Perhaps they have been written about, but I have not been able to find them.   So I set about to fill the gaps, not to write poetry, as that is quite beyond my capabilities, but I do enjoy making up what I call ditties or doggerel verse.

Mine however were so awful beside the real poems, that I thought it was better to go the whole hog, and write the lot, and compete with McGonagall for composing really bad verse.

However with a lot of assistance from Grandpa who had to completely rewrite some of them, I think we have managed to get one for each flower in this book, except for one or two where I had not left enough room to write them in.

So enjoy this book, laugh occasionally and learn a little bit too.

Grandma

is for **AVENS**

Wood, Water, and Mountain

So we start this ABC, with three flowers all called Avens, but all very different. They all belong to the Rose family, known as Rosaceae, pronounced ROSE-A-SAY. Let us take them one by one :-

Wood Avens - Geum urbanum, which you see above, is the most common of the three Avens, and is often called Herb Bennet, which comes from the old french "herbe benedicta", meaning blessed herb. It was said to repel all evil and its five petals to represent the five wounds of Jesus. Its roots are still used today in herbal medicine, and ideally, for best effect, so legend has it, should be dug up on the 25th March, — Grandpa's birthday.

The **Water Aven** - Geum rivale is the dusky member of the family, which you can see on the far right of the opposite page. It likes nice damp places to grow, it has lovely fluffy seed heads, it is rarer than the Wood Aven but has the same medical qualities.

The **Mountain Aven** Dryas octopetala is the loveliest and the rarest of all the Avens. It is very rare in fact and only grows in the West Highlands and on the Burren in West Ireland, so do not pick it if you ever find it. It is one of the European plants which got left behind after the last ice age, thousands of years ago, when we got seperated from the Mainland of Europe by the English Channel. Because its leaves resemble oak leaves, it got its latin name from the wood nymph of the oaks, called Dryad.

In the years of the ice, I was born — so shy.
I still hide from man, in the wild — alone,
Under open skies, where curlews cry,
And stonechats flit from stone to stone.

Close to the sea, midst peat and rock,
Where mountain streams and bogs abound
And rain sweeps down the near by loch,
Here I grow on secret ground.

Mountain Aven painted on the Burren 1980 and
Water Aven collected from the front of Old Allangrange

B

is for Bluebell

Campanula rotundiflora

Which belongs to the family Campanulacae - CAM-PAN-U-LAYSEA.
This is the true Bluebell of Scotland.   It is a beautiful,
delicate and fine little flower, and has always been connected with
the fairies or the little people as they are known.
What has the hare to do with the bluebell? — The English seem
to think it has some connection, as they call it the Harebell,
and call the Wild Hyacinth a bluebell.   Well the hare
has always been known as a bewitched animal and just a
little mad.   But I will tell you a little story about the
hare and the Bluebell.

      Once upon a time there was a little Bluebell who
lived just beside a dyke, and on one side of the dyke there
was a little track, and on the other side there was a big
big moor which stretched for miles.
Bluebell loved living here, sometimes she gazed over the
moor, to the purple heather, and sometimes she turned her
head looked up and down the track, and saw the occasional
person pass by, or more often the odd rabbit or bird.
She was always at her happiest in August, when she was
looking her blue-est and the sun shone.
      One hot day in August, she was gazing across the
moor when she heard a lot of loud bangs which rather frightened
her.

Picked up backroad to Allangrange Sept 78.

Suddenly a little brown hare came running towards her very fast and he seemed very out of breath and very scared. He jumped the dyke and hid behind it, just beside her.   After a little time when he had recovered his breath, they began to talk together, and he told her he was Harry the Hare, and he was very frightened as a lot of men had been walking over the moor, driving all before them including himself, and more men with guns had been shooting at the grouse who also lived on the moor.   Harry said he was not too upset about the grouse being chased a bit, as he thought it would do them no harm, as they were very grand and supercilious, and took great pride in the fact that they were real game and he was only a hare. Harry could not see why this mattered and was rather glad he was only a hare especially today.

   After this Harry and Bluebell became great friends and he used to visit her every day and sit beside her in the sun, and they enjoyed each other.   Bluebell used to tell him all about her numerous family who surrounded her, and Harry used to tell her where he had been, and what it was like the other side of the moor, where she could not see.

   Then the days grew shorter, and the weather got colder, the heather died and Bluebell told Harry that she would not be there much longer, as she disappeared in the winter when it was cold.   Harry was very sad and said he would be very lonely _ and so he was.

   One winters day when it was very cold and the moor was covered in snow, men again came out on the hill with guns, but this time, it was not the grouse they chased, but poor Harry, who showed up horribly in the snow.   He dashed away when he saw them coming and hid behind the dyke, where Bluebell lived.   But of course she was not there, and Harry was very frightened and miserable, and lay and shivered and cried.

Suddenly he felt he was not alone and felt a little less sad. Then as the light began to fade, he saw a little figure close beside him and a gentle voice told him not to be afraid. His fear had left him. He wondered who she was as she didn't look like a fairy as she was rather tubby, but she did have wings and looked a

little like a Bumble Bee. She knew what he was thinking, so told him that she was a fairy, but was a sensible one and always wore a fur coat when it was cold, and did not see why she should look "airy fairie" all the time and have cold toes.

She seemed very kind and comforting, and Harry told her all his troubles and how sad it was that there was no Bluebell to talk to and comfort him. The little person told him she would try and help him. She could not bring Bluebell back now as she would die of cold, but she could help him, and she would change the colour of his coat to white, so he would not show up in the snow, and when the Spring came it would become blue grey to match Bluebell.

Harry thanked her very much and she disappeared, but his coat was still the same colour, which was disappointing, but as he was very tired he went to sleep just where he was.

However the next morning, when he woke he had a glorious snow white coat, and Oh he was so thrilled. He dashed off over the moor through the snow, and those horrid men couldn't see him.

All winter he ran about in the snow and was quite safe, then gradually the days got longer and the sun got warmer, and his lovely white coat of which he was so proud, changed slowly to a beautiful silver blue. He used to come back daily to the dyke to see if Bluebell had come back, and then one lovely day
- There she was —

Oh they were happy to be together again, and they had so much to tell eachother and Harry told all that had happened and all about the Fairy and his lovely white coat and his new silver blue one.

They had a lovely Summer and the next year when Bluebell left, and Harry's coat turned white again, he was not so unhappy as he realized he would see her again. The only thing that made Harry a little sad was that Bluebell always disappeared before his coat turned white so she could never see it.

So now you know when you see a Blue Mountain Hare why it is blue, and why it turns white in the winter.

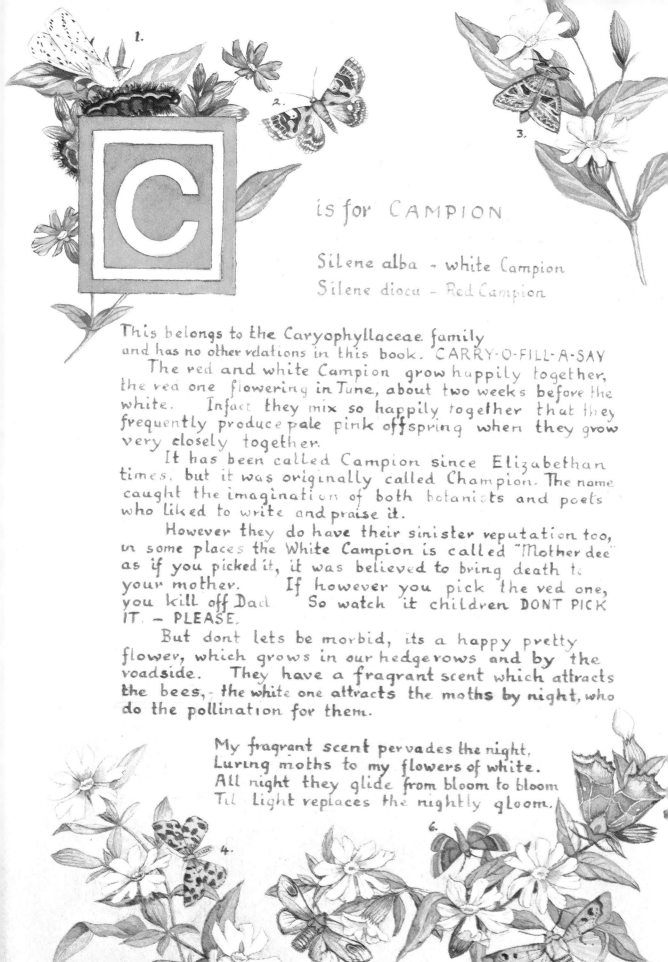

C is for CAMPION

Silene alba - white Campion
Silene dioca - Red Campion

This belongs to the Caryophyllaceae family
and has no other relations in this book. CARRY-O-FILL-A-SAY
The red and white Campion grow happily together,
the red one flowering in June, about two weeks before the
white. Infact they mix so happily together that they
frequently produce pale pink offspring when they grow
very closely together.

It has been called Campion since Elizabethan
times, but it was originally called Champion. The name
caught the imagination of both botanists and poets
who liked to write and praise it.

However they do have their sinister reputation too,
in some places the White Campion is called "Mother dee"
as if you picked it, it was believed to bring death to
your mother. If however you pick the red one,
you kill off Dad So watch it children DONT PICK
IT. - PLEASE.

But dont lets be morbid, its a happy pretty
flower, which grows in our hedgerows and by the
roadside. They have a fragrant scent which attracts
the bees, - the white one attracts the moths by night, who
do the pollination for them.

My fragrant scent pervades the night,
Luring moths to my flowers of white.
All night they glide from bloom to bloom
Til light replaces the nightly gloom.

Turn to end of book for details of Moths

Collected from roadside going to Munlochy June 80

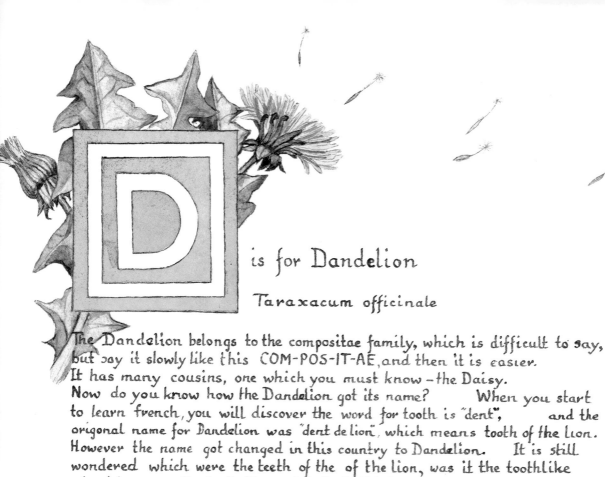

D is for Dandelion

Taraxacum officinale

The Dandelion belongs to the compositae family, which is difficult to say, but say it slowly like this COM-POS-IT-AE, and then it is easier. It has many cousins, one which you must know – the Daisy. Now do you know how the Dandelion got its name? When you start to learn french, you will discover the word for tooth is "dent", and the origonal name for Dandelion was "dent de lion", which means tooth of the lion. However the name got changed in this country to Dandelion. It is still wondered which were the teeth of the of the lion, was it the toothlike edged leaves, or the tooth like petals? I think the petals, because who ever heard of a lion with green teeth! The Dandelion is also known as the childrens clock, because of the game of puffing away the feathery seedheads. The number of puffs supposedly gives the hour.

I am a Dandelion, with teeth of gold,
And grow most places where I'm told,
And many where I'm not!
My feathery seed by the wind is fanned
Over all the countryside and land
And into your garden plot.
But I make amends in April and May,
When I am lovely beside the Motorway
So please dont say I'm not.

I picked this dandelion in June 78 in Dillington farmyard

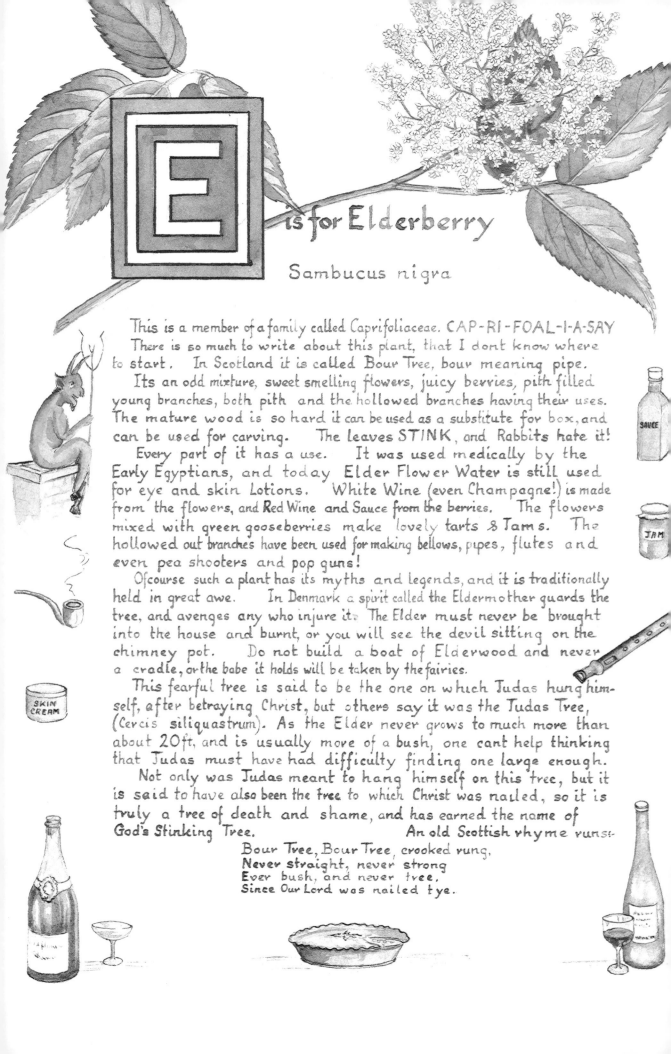

E is for Elderberry

Sambucus nigra

This is a member of a family called Caprifoliaceae. CAP-RI-FOAL-I-A-SAY
There is so much to write about this plant, that I dont know where to start.   In Scotland it is called Bour Tree, bour meaning pipe.

Its an odd mixture, sweet smelling flowers, juicy berries, pith filled young branches, both pith and the hollowed branches having their uses. The mature wood is so hard it can be used as a substitute for box, and can be used for carving.   The leaves STINK, and Rabbits hate it!

Every part of it has a use.   It was used medically by the Early Egyptians, and today Elder Flower Water is still used for eye and skin Lotions.   White Wine (even Champagne!) is made from the flowers, and Red Wine and Sauce from the berries.   The flowers mixed with green gooseberries make lovely tarts & Jams.   The hollowed out branches have been used for making bellows, pipes, flutes and even pea shooters and pop guns!

Ofcourse such a plant has its myths and legends, and it is traditionally held in great awe.   In Denmark a spirit called the Eldermother guards the tree, and avenges any who injure it. The Elder must never be brought into the house and burnt, or you will see the devil sitting on the chimney pot.   Do not build a boat of Elderwood and never a cradle, or the babe it holds will be taken by the fairies.

This fearful tree is said to be the one on which Judas hung himself, after betraying Christ, but others say it was the Judas Tree, (Cercis siliquastrum). As the Elder never grows to much more than about 20ft, and is usually more of a bush, one cant help thinking that Judas must have had difficulty finding one large enough.

Not only was Judas meant to hang himself on this tree, but it is said to have also been the tree to which Christ was nailed, so it is truly a tree of death and shame, and has earned the name of God's Stinking Tree.   An old Scottish rhyme runs:

Bour Tree, Bour Tree, crooked rung,
Never straight, never strong
Ever bush, and never tree,
Since Our Lord was nailed tye.

I collected this elder in the hedge of Aunt Kirstie's
house in Plymouth in Oct 78

F is for Forget-me-Not

Mysotis scoriodes

This belongs to the Boraginaceae family, and it has no relations in this book. (BOR-AT-IN-A-SAY)

But how did this flower get the name "Forget-me-Not?" Well there is the well known story of the lovers walking by the Danube, and how the young man plunged & swam to an island where the maiden had spied some blue flowers she fancied. How he got cramp on the homeward swim, and he was carried away in the current. He threw her the flowers calling "Forget me Not."

The story which I like however, is the one about Adam, how he named all the flowers in the garden of Eden, but is believed to have overlooked this little flower. After he had given each flower a name, he took a walk all around the garden, calling each flower by their new names to see if they all consented. It was really a kind of Roll Call, or like 'Bill' at Harrow, which you two boys will know about when you go there.

He had nearly finished his walk around, when a little voice said "What about me Adam, what is my name?" Adam was very upset at having missed this beautiful little flower, and not naming it. So he said "I forgot you before, I shall name you in a way I shall never forget you again "Forget me Not."

The flower pictured here is the Water Forget me Not, named after a scorpion as the young flowers uncurl like a scorpions tail.

EC.80

Collected from the burn behind Munlochy Post Office 23 July 80

G

is for Geranium sylvaticum

Wood Cranesbill

It belongs to the Geraniacea family, who we have not met before. GER-AN-I-AY-SAY.

This time, I have put the Latin name first, because it is a very well known word which we all use. The word geranium comes from the Greek word "geranos" which means crane. So this is the reason we call all our native geraniums - Cranesbills. The reason the Greeks called the geranium after this bird, is because its fruit, which comes after the flower, looks very like a cranes beak or bill. We seldom see cranes here, as they dont live here, but they do sometimes land, when blown off course, flying from Scandinavia to Spain and further south.

The Wood Cranesbill we show opposite, is one of many, and grows mostly in Scotland. Another well known one which grows almost every where, is called Herb Robert, or sometimes unkindly Stinking Cranesbill. and is the only one of medical value, but who Robert was no one seems able to decide. Some say Robin Goodfellow, some say Robin Hood, and some say St.Robert, the founder of the Cistercian Monks. So take your pick.

My garden relations get drilled in a bed,
Of delphiniums blue and geraniums red.
But I'm the cousin who likes to hide
In a hedge or a bank, or woodland ride.
Us country blokes get another name,
They call us after the beak of a crane.
But I dont think I look like a bird,
And find the idea all quite absurd.

Geranium robertianum.

EC. 80

Glen Fargue
16ᵗʰ June 80

H is for Heather

Calluna vulgaris

The name of the family is Ericaceae – ERIC-A-SAY, not too bad to say. Now the word Heather comes from an old Teutonic word for waste-land – Heath, and the people who lived in this heathland were called "heathens". As these people usually lived in remote places, they were the last to be converted to Christianity, which is why we now use the word for non-Christians.

However the people of Scotland were Christian from a very early age, though they lived with the heather & depended on it for their livelihood. They built their houses with it, they thatched their houses with it, they made heather beds to sleep on, and they made it into brooms to clean the house. And when the heather died it helped make the peat which they depended on for fuel to burn. So you see it was very important in these olden days. As for today – read this:-

In these modern times, I have uses still.
My flowers cover both the moor and the hill,
To the joy of the tourist with their "oohs" and "aahs"
Who come in their buses and moter cars.
They collect me in armfuls but not to make brooms,
But just to adorn their suburban rooms.
Though I am no longer of use in the house
I'm the main source of food for the sheep and the grouse,
But for poor little me, those great men of wealth
Could never enjoy their "Glorious Twelfth".

The Emperor Moth
which lives in the heather.

E.C.

I picked this in September on the moor behind
Allangrange

I is for Ivy-leaved Toadflax

Cymbalaria muralis

I am very sorry this plant has a terrible family name Scrophulariacea, what a mouthful for such a small flower, but if you say it like this its not so hard SCROF-U-LAR-I-A-SEA.   It has some extrodinary cousins which belong to the same family, the foxglove and the Verbascum, which you will come across later in this book.   How odd that something so small and something so large as a Verbascum should be cousins. Now why was this little flower called Toadflax?   Well the other flax's are very useful plants–either they can be used for medecine or can be woven into cloth. But this little flower is pretty & charming, but has no uses, and someone is reputed to have said "Its a flax only fit for toads".

> I am a small little plant of lilac and white.
> And I creep about stones all day and all night.
> They say that I'm useless, and my habits are lax,
> That I'm neither an ivy nor am I a flax.
> So my name seems misleading as you've been told,
> But Heaven forbid I should look like a toad.

Poor little toad, he's not all that bad, though his looks are a little agaist him!   He is different from a frog as he has no teeth and cannot hop like a frog, and crawls about more.   Lets let him have his say

> I like dark corners, and come out at night,
> And I know that I'm not a beautiful sight,
> Though perfectly harmless, I'm terribly shy,
> And nobody loves me– I do wonder why.

I picked this flower in June on Nannies step's at Allangrange.

J

is for Jack by the Hedge

Allaria petiolata

This flower belongs to the family called Cruciferae, like the crucifix, which you know is a cross. CRU-SEE-FER-AY and a cousin, I expect you know well is the Cabbage. All the flowers in the family have four petals like a cross. Very interesting all this family is edible, though some may not taste too good. If you crush the leaves of this plant, they smell of garlic.

Again it is an important plant for the butterflies, especially the Orange Tipped one. However we meet that one later on in "L", so I show a Cabbage White here.

It is one of the first to appear green in the spring hedgerows, and though it is said to be scarce in Scotland, there is a lot of it by the road between here and Munlochy.

Why is it called Jack? Well, Jack was a common name given to describe any common friendly chap, "Any Old Jack", or "Any Jill's Jack". So a suitable name for this friendly and humble hedgerow plant.

We have told you that the cabbage is a cousin, and I wonder if you know the story why the man went to the moon because of the cabbage. He liked cabbages very much, but he had none himself, so on Christmas Eve he stole one from a neighbour. Every one was so horrified he could do such a thing on Christmas Eve, they said "Since you rob on this Holy Night let you and your basket go off to the Moon". And whisked away he was beyond temptation. But friendly Cousin Jack still stays in our hedges.

Devonians call me "Poor mans Mustard",
To eat with meat, before the custard.
In Somerset I'm "Sauce Alone",
Perhaps no 'veg' with just a bone.
Though food and drink you well may lack,
I'm always here the Friendly Jack.

From the roadside on the way to Munlochy May 79

K is for King Cup

Caltha palustris

It is a member of the Rununculaceae family, (RUN-UN-Q-LAY-SEA) and cousin to the first flower in this book the Anemone.

It makes a lovely splash of bright gold from spring to Summer in our ditches and streams, as it loves the water.

This picture of it, is of rather a late flower and a little smaller than they usually are. Perhaps because of its lovely gold colour it is said that the meaning of King Cup is a desire for riches and its motto "I wish I was rich."

It also has another name Marsh Marigold, which is odd as it is not a Marigold. Perhaps the reason for this is that the old English name for it was "Meare Meorgealle", which is Marsh Maresgall in todays spelling. Now a gall is a small blister or swelling, and horses especially suffer from this. As these galls look very like the buds of the Marsh Marigold it was called Maresgall and Marsh because it grows near water. Maresgall gradually became Marigold, just because the word sounded rather like Maresgall, and perhaps rather nicer. Incidently these tight little buds of King Cup used to be gathered and pickled, and used as capers in the old days.

Sometimes also it is called the May Flower as it comes out then. So, on May Day, this fertility Festival Day, it was much used to avert the dangers of witches and fairies who were always around in extra large crowds on this day. They used to hang the King Cup upside down in doorways to prevent the witches entering - especially in byres to prevent the cows becoming bewitched.

My sepals so bright emerge in spring
Forming a cup which is fit for a King.
My colour of gold makes me wish I was rich,
Inspite of the fact that I live in a ditch.

Collected Munlochy Bay. July 79.

L is for Lady's Smock

Cardamine pratensis

This flower is one of the Cruciferae family and has two cousins in this book, Jack by the Hedge, and the Northern Bedstraw   Pronounced CRU-SI-FUR-AY.

It has a second name by which it is equally well known, the Cuckoo Flower.   It is said to come into flower when the Cuckoo arrives, and the flowers fade when the Cuckoo ceases to sing.

Like all the cruciferae family it can be eaten, and is full of vitamin C   Its leaves can be eaten as cress, and it is one of the favourite foods of the Orange Tipped Butterfly, who do not seem to mind its rather bitter taste.

But how did the name "Lady's Smock arrive?   There are many theories, and one is that it refers to the smock of Our Lady, which she was wearing when Jesus was born. She is thought to have left it behind in a cave at Bethlehem, when she fled to Egypt.   This was later found by St Helena and it was taken to St Sophia in Byzantium, and later taken by Charlemagne to Aix-la-Chapelle, where it is worshipped as a relic.

It is meant to be unlucky to pick, as it is said if you do, you will be bitten by an adder before the year is out.   Possibly the reason for this story is because adders often liked to curl up and sleep beneath the Lady's Smock, and then possibly frightened by those collecting the flowers, let fly at them

Do not lets end the story of this flower with its unpleasant side

I open my eyes when the cuckoo arrives
And bloom as long as he survives.
Those three short months that he is here,
Are mine as well. So shed no tear
When we depart. We enjoyed our stay.
And will come again another day.

Collected this on loch Lomand side   23 April 80.

EC. 80

M is for Monkey Flower

Mimulus luteus

This belongs to the Scrophulariacea family, and amongs its cousins are the Verbascum and Speedwell. Pronounced SCROF-U-LAR-I-A-SAY.

It is called the Monkey Flower because its face is said to resemble a little grinning Monkey. There are two Monkey Flowers, Mimulus guttatus and also Mimulus luteus, both are yellow and have red spots, but I think the one here is Luteus, as it has larger red spots than guttatus. The Scottish call it "Blood drop emlet" as they thought the flowers resembled a little helmet upside down.

The first of these flowers were introduced in 1812 from the Aleutian Islands off Alaska, where it was nearly always foggy and can rain for 250 days in the year. It became a popular garden flower, but by 1824 it had escaped first into Wales and then all over the country. It rushed along streams and waterways, and cheered the drabness of industrial sites. It obviously thought our climate was wonderful compared with the Aleutian Islands.

The other Mimulus came from Chile, but it had not been here long, before this escaped also, and made its way over the country, mostly to the North.

Obviously the Mimulus is a plant of freedom and does not approve of being restricted or fenced in,

I was glad to escape from those wet northern Isles,
To be here, where the sun occasionally smiles.
I was glad to be able your gardens to grace
To smile upon you, with my monkeylike face.
But I felt walled up, which I started to hate,
So made an escape through the old garden gate.
I wandered so far, by rivers and streams,
Until I had found the land of my dreams.
So thats why I'm here by Loch Tummel side,
I have come a long way, but here I shall bide.

Picked from ditch by the side of Loch Tummel 12 June 80

N is for Northern Bedstraw

Galium Boreale

This belongs to the family called Rubiaceae RU-BI-A-SAY There are quite a lot of different bedstraws, they are all quite common little flowers, and most of them are white like this one here, which is the one that grows in the north.

In the very old days, before they had mattresses, they used to sleep on straw. However straw in those days did not necessarily mean what we call straw today, it really referred to any dried plant suitable to sleep on. It was usually a mixture of bracken and this little flower which is sweet when it is dried.

The Legend says, when Jesus was born the Virgin Mary was lying on a bed of bracken and bedstraw, like many people did. The bracken refused to acknowledge the child, and has lost its flower, and has never flowered since. The Bedstraw welcomed the child, and at that moment found its flowers had turned from white to gold. So this bedstraw is called "Lady's Bedstraw and has lovely yellow flowers. I don't think our little Northern Bedstraw could have been there as it is still white.

Bedstraw was also used in the old days as rennet to curdle the milk for cheese making.

Long ago in that Eastern Stable,
I was laid in the babies cradle.
It was for me, my greatest hour,
And such an honour for my flower.
But greater sights were to unfold,
My flowers of white did turn to gold.

The Fungi in the picture opposite is Lactaries rufus, Red Milk Cap. It was growing in the pinewoods near the Bedstraw

EL. 80

Collected by the pinewoods behind Allangrange   August 80

is for Ox-eye Daisy

Leucanthemum vulgare

This large Daisy belongs to the Compositae family (COM-POS-IT-AY) like all daisies.   As its latin name suggests it is a Chrysanthemum and a cousin of all those glamorous flowers which we see in shops and houses in the early winter.   If you look at the leaves, you will see the likeness.

It is also known as the Moon Daisy, and in some places the Dunder Daisy, as it was said to keep Thunder at bay;   You hung up a bunch of these daisies on the roof of your house or byre which you wished to protect.   It was named "Ox-eye" by Discordes the Greek in the first century, a long time ago! It also had herbal values, but it is not one of our greatest medical herbs. John Plechy said that if you drunk a concoction of this plant, it would cure all diseases caused by drinking cold beer when you were hot.

However this flower even if it does not rank very highly as a herb, brings much brightness and cheerfulness to our hedgerows.   How it glows out at us, which perhaps may cause us to think that Moon Daisy is not such a bad name for it after all.   It is also known for the age old game of pulling off the petals one by one saying "he loves me, he loves me not, he loves me, he loves me not", hoping it ends up "he loves me".

Perhaps the modern "Miss" could re-write the old song a little

Daisy Daisy, give me your answer do
I'm half crazy, but is he really true!
I don't want a stylish marriage,
And perish the thought of a carriage,
But what I'd like,
Is not a bike
But a sports car just for two

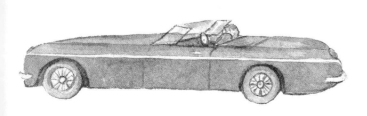

P is for PANSY

Viola tricolor

The Pansy belongs to the Violaceae family (VI-OL-A-SEA) & is a cousin to all the violets, and this humble little wild flower is the ancestor of all those glorious big pansies we grow in our gardens.

The French people call this flower "Pensée" which means thought, and the English called it the same, but gradually pensee got changed to pansy.   So its a thoughtful little flower, and William Shakespeare wrote in Hamlet:-

> There's rosemary, thats for remembrance: pray
> love, remember: and there is pansies thats for
> thought.

The pansy is also called Heartsease, as in olden days, doctors made a medicine of this flower, which was good for complaints of the heart.   I think it must have also been good for the heartache of lovers, as locally it earned such names as "Kiss me Quick" and "Kiss me at the Garden Gate"   In fact in the play "Midsummer Night's Dream" Oberon squeezes the juices from the Heartsease into Titania's eyes, so she would fall in love with Bottom the ass.   Shakespeare obviously enjoyed this little flower.

It grows in dry and sunny places, on grassland and waste land, and its flowers vary a lot in both size and colours as can be seen from the faces above and below.

> I love you for the thoughts you bring,
> Of which the greatest poets sing.
> I love the way you ease our heart
> When it is struck by Cupid's dart
> I love you for your style and grace
> Whats more I love your silly face.

Picked on the Leanach   June 78

is for Quercus

which is the Latin name for Oak.

Lots of little boys and girls know an oak tree, but very few know its Latin name Quercus, so you are very special now you know.   Oak trees grow very big and live for a very long time.   They say they take 200 years to grow up, then live for 200 years grown up, and then take another 200 years to die, so they see many changes in their life time.   This tree saw your great grandfather going through the Park in a horse and carriage, and I am very much afraid it will live to see a motorway skirting the Park.

The oak was very important in olden days, before ships were built of steel, as all the ships of our navy, which guarded our Island were built with wood from the oak tree.   Also it was used to build houses like yours with its oak beams, and the acorns were eaten by the pigs, which fed under all the oaks in the Park.

I have seen many a change from where I stand
In Dillington Park, on this fertile land.
I've seen Hannings and Vaughan-Lee's come and go,
Now Camerons are here to harvest and sow.
And I'll still be here in two thousand and ten,
When Jamie and Ewenie are hard working men.

Quercus the oak lives at Dillington Park
It has acorns galore and a crinkly bark.
The acorn when planted
As your children will see,
Will one day grow into a beautiful tree.

EC 1980

I collected these leaves and acorns from the first tree on the left
when you enter the Park from the farmhouse.

R is for Rose

Rosa canina

This belongs to the Rosaceae (ROSE-A-SAY) family and is a cousin of that curious little flower, the Tormantil.

Roses have been grown down the ages, both for medical purposes and just for delight. It has a lovely scent, is beautiful to look at, and at the end of the season it has lovely red hips, which are used to make the rose hip syrup which is so good for you.

The Rose is loved by all the world, and it is a symbol of so many things, has been written about and painted so often, and has many times played its part in history, such as the Wars of the Roses, and this following story:-

To say something is Sub Rosa, implies it is a secret. This dates from 427 B.C, when the Spartans and the Athenians were intrigueing with Xerxes, the Persian, to hand Greece over to the Emperor. The meeting was held under a bower of roses near The Temple of Minerva. As it was held in such secrecy, other such meetings were referred to as Sub Rosa. That is why one often has a plaster rose decorating the centre of dining rooms and conference chambers, implying what you hear or learn there, is private and not to be passed on.

Hush, Hush, Hush, you are under the rose,
You may know something which nobody knows,
About somebody, or about something
But to your secret you must cling
Your lips are sealed, you cannot speak,
And only mischief makers squeak.

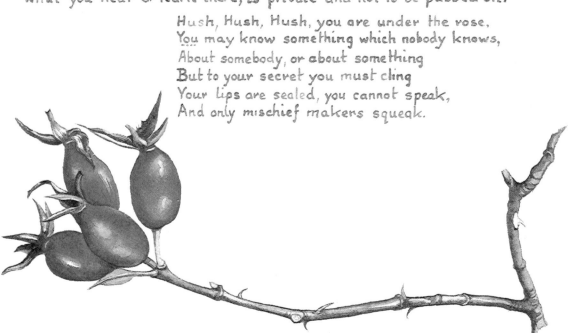

Collected from bush on the corner on back road to Allangrange 17 July 79

S is for Sneezewort

Achillea ptarmica

is also for Speedwell

Veronica chamaedrys

We have two flowes for "S" so I will start with the Sneezewort.
This belongs to the Compositae (COM-POS-IT-AY) family and has
two cousins in this book, the dandelion and the Yarrow.

How did it get the name Sneezewort? Well it is said if you dry
the flowers and grind them into a powder and sniff it like snuff you will
sneeze. I am sure you would, you could'nt help it, and I can't help
thinking that if you treated other flowers the same way, it would have
the same effect. It is sometimes known as devils pepper.

Now the Speedwell belongs to the Scrophulariaceae family,
(SCROF-U-LAR-I-A-SEA) the same as the Ivy Leaved Toadflax.
Its latin name Veronica, is after the Saint of that name.

The Early Christian Legend tells us how St Veronica stepped from
the crowd watching Jesus stagger those last painful steps to Calvary,
and took her handkerchief, and wiped the blood and sweat from his
brow. The handkerchief was said to be immediatly imprinted
with the Divine features and became a relic. St. Veronica is said
to have liked the "true blue" colour of the Speedwell, and taken it for her
own, and to be the emblem of Womans Fidelity.

The English name Speedwell, rather tells its own story. It
is said that to carry or wear it on a journey, brought you good
luck. In Ireland travellers would sew sprigs of this flower to their
clothing to ward off accidents on their journey and to assure their
safe return.

> In olden days, the roads were rough,
> To go on a journey, you had to be tough.
> On lonely tracks, or through dark woods
> The Highwayman stole your worldy goods
> The coaches were cold, you often got stuck
> So travellers took me with them for luck.
>
> But no one wants my help these days
> Inspite of the "pile ups" on motorways.
> No thought of me when they're up in the sky
> Being "Highjacked" perhaps, enroute to Dubai,
> So if all these dangers you would dispel,
> Please take me with you, I'll speed you well.

Picked both these flowers up the back road behind Allangrange 14ᵗʰ Aug 79

T is for Trientalis europea

Chickweed   Wintergreen (English name)

T is for Tormentil

Potentilla erecta   (Latin name)

On this page we again have two flowers. and I shall write about the Trientalis.   It belongs to the Primulaceae family, PRIM-U-LACE-AY. and is the cousin of the Cowslip and the Primrose.

It grows mostly up here in the Highlands and it is not very often found growing in England.   It likes to grow in mossy pine woods, and as can be seen. is a dainty little flower.   Apart from this. I really do not know much about it, all the herb books, and reference books on flower names. totally ignore it. so it is a neglected little flower.

The Tormentil on the other hand, we do know a little about.   You would not think it, but it belongs to the same family as the rose. Rosaceae, ROSA-SAY.   The name is adapted from the Latin word Tormentilla, which means the torment plant.   The roots. which contain tannin are prescribed for griping stomach pains and the torment of toothache. The roots also give out a red dye and they can be used as tannin and a substitute for tannin bark.   In the Western Isles, the fishermen used to tan their nets with the roots.

I'm a Trientalis and grow in the North,
You seldom see me south of the Forth.
I have no history, or story to tell,
I can neither cure you, or weave a spell
But Sassenachs find me rare and strange,
When they seek my flowers at Allangrange.

Picked both these flowers behind Allangrang in August 1979

is for Ulex europaeus

Gorse, Furze or Whins.

This plant belongs to the Leguminosae family, which is the same family as the pea you eat. Pronounced LEG-OOM-IN-O-SAY

It has three common names, Gorse, which is used all over the country, Furze or Fuzz in the south and Whins in the north.

In the old days they used to crush the prickly spikes and feed it to stock, and they also make wine from the flowers.

It is the flower however of enduring affection, and a great favourite with lovers. The saying goes "Love is out of season, when the Fuzz is out of blossom. However it very seldom is, as there are several different species, which all flower at different times of the year, so there is nearly always a flower in bloom. "Blossom time is Kissing time".

There is no more glorious sight in spring, than a hillside covered with gorse in flower. When Linnaeus the great botanist came to England in 1736 and saw the lovely flowers of the gorse covering Putney Common, he fell on his knees and thanked God for its beauty. Perhaps in Sweden, where he lived the frosts were too hard to allow it to flower in such profusion, as the gorse does suffer and gets cut back by the frost.

I am a flower of joy and not of gloom,
Its kissing time when I'm in bloom
I flower when Spring is in the air,
When man and beast begin to pair.
I'm due in March, should end in June,
Though lovers find this far too soon.
Lucky for them, I'm never on time,
I'm early and late, and thats no crime.

EC. 80

Picked on the backroad to Allangrange 26ᵗʰ May 80.

V is for Verbascum

which is the latin name for Aaron's Rod or Mullein

It belongs to the family of Scrophlariaceae (SCROF-U-LAR-I-A-SEA), so has several cousins in this book who you have already met, the Ivy Leafed Toadflax, and the Monkey Flower. Another tall cousin, who I think you must know is the fox glove

It is a very tall flower 4-6ft high, much taller than you are (now!) and has lovely soft hairy leaves. Because of this it is often called locally such names as Flannel Flower, Blanket Leaf and even Bunny ears. Because in the old days people used to dip the tall stems in pitch and use them as candles, it was also called the Candlewick plant.

However by far the most popular name is Aaron's Rod. We learn in the Bible that Moses told the Israelite families to each place their rods before Gods tabernacle, and God would give a sign as who was to be the chosen leader. The next day when Moses returned to the tabernacle he found that Aaron's Rod had blossomed and later produced almonds, to show he was the chosen one. (Legend does not explain how a verbascum produced almonds, so dont ask!)

I am a tall & golden wasteland flower,
But in Moses day, I had my hour.
Infact its odd,
To think that God,
Used common me to help select,
Aaron for his priest elect.

Picked by bridge, Munlochy Bay

July 79

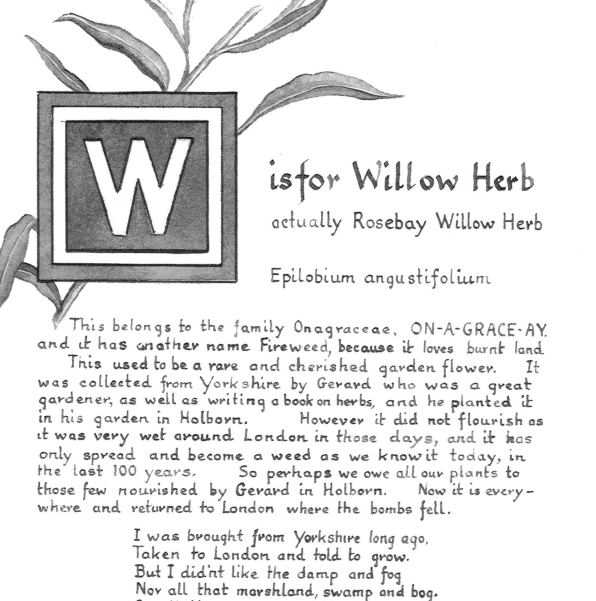

W is for Willow Herb

actually Rosebay Willow Herb

Epilobium angustifolium

This belongs to the family Onagraceae, ON-A-GRACE-AY. and it has another name Fireweed, because it loves burnt land.
This used to be a rare and cherished garden flower. It was collected from Yorkshire by Gerard who was a great gardener, as well as writing a book on herbs, and he planted it in his garden in Holborn. However it did not flourish as it was very wet around London in those days, and it has only spread and become a weed as we know it today, in the last 100 years. So perhaps we owe all our plants to those few nourished by Gerard in Holborn. Now it is every-where and returned to London where the bombs fell.

I was brought from Yorkshire long ago,
Taken to London and told to grow.
But I did'nt like the damp and fog
Nor all that marshland, swamp and bog.
So all those years while it was wet,
I just remained a garden pet.

When modern ways took life in hand
And draining changed the marsh to land
The country laid with railway track,
And factories made the Country black.
I loved it all, and wished to thrive,
And suddenly became alive.

I threw my seed both far and wide
And lept around the countryside.
And later during the london blitz
When much of it was blown to bits
I made a come back just to cheer
The bombed out Cockney from his fear.

Outside studio window   29ᵗʰ August 79

X is for extra

and I have chosen HAWTHORN

Crataegus monoyma praecox

This belongs to the Rosaceae family which we have met already.

The tree, I am writing about, is the "Glastonbury Thorn." It is said that when St Joseph of Aramathaea visited England and came to Glastonbury, he liked it so much that he stuck his staff into the ground, saying "Here I wish to stay" The staff took root and grew · This tree flowers in the winter and not in May, as do most other thorn trees, which is why they are also known as May Trees.

Why I have chosen this thorn as our extra is because it has a special connection with Dillington. It was said that there were two origonal cuttings from that Holy Thorn at Glastonbury, one was planted in the front Park at Dillington and one I believe in the Botanical Gardens, Edinburgh. As a small girl I remember this tree, old and bent, and slightly more pink than the one painted opposite. The local legend was that it blossomed on Christmas Eve, and on that night the cattle knelt down before it. Alas in my day no cattle were allowed in the front Park, by my Father, so I could never prove this! Now they have cattle there, but not the thorn tree, as it finally toppled over in the twenties. So I shall just go on believing that they did kneel to our tree - its such a nice thought. I dont think the other cutting could prove eit either as I have never heard of cattle roaming in a botanical garden!

As a first child of that Thorn on Glastonbury Tor,
I was honored by man and held in great awe,
And soon became known as the Dillington Thorn.
So centuries went by, and new centuries were born,
But mankind soon forgets — When I finally fell
Few minded or cared. nor my legend could tell.

But all through those years I had one glorious hour,
On each Christmas Eve. I came into flower
And the beasts of the field all gathered around.
And knelt by my side on the frost covered ground,
As they humbly knelt I was filled with great love
For that babe which has brought such light from above.

Y

is for Yellow Iris

Iris pseudacorus

This flower belongs to the Iridacae (IRI-DAY-SAY) family.

Our yellow Iris is one of the most beautiful and stately of wild flowers, fit to grace any garden, and yet it grows in damp places all over our land. Its other names are Yellow Flag, Fleur de Luce and Segg. Segg is an old Saxon name for a dagger, because of its sword like leaves, it got this name, and also the names of Dagger and Jacobs Sword in some places.

The Iris has for long been connected with the Kings of France, where it also grows abundantly. The story goes that Clovis, an early Frankish King, whose emblem was three toads was not having great success in battle until his wife Clotilde, who was a Christian, presented him with a new shield, with 3 irises painted on as an emblem. His luck changed, he started to win battles, and became a Christian, I think in that order. Some say this story is nonsence and that the emblem was always an Iris, but was so badly painted that they looked like toads! However Louis VII took the Iris 600 years later as his emblem in the Crusades, and it became known as Fleur de Louis. Later the Iris changed into a lily to become the Fleur-de-Lis. Toad to Iris, Iris to Lily? I always thought the French could paint !

Once an emblem of the Kings in the earlys days of France,
When my three flowers replaced that curious little toad.
I was borne to distant lands on many a shield and lance.
But I prefer old soggy England, and its ditches by the road.

Here I bring bright light and joy to many a shady place,
With my toes in watery meadows, where rushes grow & thrive.
My tall and sword like leaves spear the air with grace
And my flag flowers send the signal "How good to be alive"

Z is for Zenry

Somerset for Charlock

Sinapsis arvensis

I am ending this book and Alphabet with a common weed, which is about all anyone has to say about this flower. In fact the only reason I include it here, is because of the old Somerset name for it, "Zenry".   There are very few flowers which start with the letter Z.

It belongs to the Cruciferae family (CRUS-IF-FUR-AY) and like all members of that family it can be eaten. However most people can find better things to eat as a vegetable than this plant, though it is much liked by cattle and sheep. It does bring us pleasure, when it grows en masse in a field, more than likely where its not meant to be, and produces a lovely streak of bright yellow across the sunlit countryside.

Zenry or Charlock which is its usual name, is one of the mustards, and its seeds can be ground down to make the mustard we eat with our sausages.   However it does not make such good mustard as the one especially grown for the purpose.

In fact it is not a popular plant at all and was once referred to as the vegetable rat!   Poor little Zenry.

And whats wrong with being a rat?

Farmers and gardeners are agreed
That I'm an obnoxious and odious weed.
They try to kill me with their spray.
I'd not be here if they had their way.
So if I'm ever to survive
I must fight to stay alive.
I fear I lack all earthly charm,
But really I do little harm
So shed a tear, where'er you be
And some one, please think well of me.
Perhaps the great God up above
Will pity me, whom none can love.

Picked near Padstow, Cornwall   5th March!

Moths on the "C" page

I introduced a few moths on this page, as I thought before I did so, it was rather uninteresting. I would like to point out however, only No 3, the Campion Moth lives and lay their eggs on the Campion. They are all depicted with the Campion on this page, just for artistic purposes only.

No 1. White Ermine. A moth of gardens and open country, flies by night. Deposits her eggs on Dandelion, Dock and low plants.

No 2. Mother Shipton. So called because it resembles a wizened old woman. Flies by day, lays eggs on Clovers.

No 3. The Campion likes open country, flies after dark. Lays eggs on the bladder campion.

No 4. Speckled Yellow. Flies by day through woodlands. Larvae feed on wood sage, woundworts and dead nettles.

No 5. Pebble Prominent. A common night flying moth. Deposits eggs, and larvae feed, on food plants.

No 6. Small Purple-barred. A night flying moth, which lives where the milkwort grows.

No 7. Lesser Yellow Underwing. Flies by night and lays its eggs on various grasses and other plants.

No 8. The Herald. A moth which looks like a shrivelled leaf when resting during the day. Visits ivy in the autumn, and sallows in spring. Lays eggs on sallows, willows and poplars.